Learning Cohort 3

The
Nearness
of God

Forty Days With Dallas Willard

Andrew Barrett, Bohye Kim,
and Spencer Engelke

Table of Contents

ii

Abbreviations

RH   Willard, Dallas. *Renovation of the Heart: Putting on the Character of Christ.* Colorado Springs: NavPress, 2002.

DC   Willard, Dallas. *The Divine Conspiracy: Rediscovering Our Hidden Life in God.* San Francisco: HarperSanFrancisco, 1997.

SD   Willard, Dallas. *The Spirit of the Disciplines: Understanding How God Changes Lives.* San Francisco: HarperSanFrancisco, 1988.

Authors' Introduction

Over the course of the Spring 2019 semester at George W. Truett Theological Seminary, we participated in a practical theology course on the life and work of Dallas Willard (1935-2013). One of the assignments for the class was for the three of us to write a forty-day devotional based on Willard's work. We found such an assignment to be a genuine pleasure, because not only were we being formed personally by Willard's work, but we were given an opportunity to take what we were learning and experiencing and utilize it all in the writing of this book.

We decided to center our book around the nearness of God and his kingdom to us today. By the life and ministry of Christ, the kingdom of God is available *right now* for all who would place their confidence in him as their master. Each of the contributions are built around this theme in some way, shape, or form. Our aim was to both compel the reader to realize just how near God's kingdom is *and* to draw attention to the way participation in that kingdom should shape our lives.

What we offer here is not the work of three begrudged seminary students. This is the work of three people who, captivated by the work of this man, are thinking through Scripture afresh and sharing what they are learning in these devotionals. The reflections shared in our devotionals are often derived from what was taking place in our personal spiritual lives as a result of this course. With that in mind, it is our genuine hope that the reader will join us in our captivation with this man's work. We hope that our work will be an encouragement to the reader, and that they will be compelled to read more of Willard's work. Our ultimate hope, however, is that the reader will realize that God and his kingdom are *near* and *available,* calling us to live a new kind of life with our heavenly Father.

Sincerely,

Andrew Barrett, Bohye Kim, and Spencer Engelke

THE PROLEM OF OVERFAMILIARITY
John 14:6-9
Andrew Barrett

"The major problem with the invitation [to the life of God] now is precisely overfamiliarity... People think they have heard the invitation. They think they have accepted it – or rejected it. But they have not."
(DC, 11)

Much has occurred between the beginning of John's Gospel and Chapter 14. Through the inclusion of miracles, OT echoes, discourses, and human-interaction, John brilliantly communicates that in Christ the Father has become flesh and is inaugurating his kingdom on earth as in heaven. Within this inaugural movement is the invitation for God's sheep to step through the door into life with their good shepherd (cf. Jn. 10.7-18). While readers might suppose that the disciples understood what this life looked like, the chilling reality is that Philip, despite having been with Jesus for a long time, still did not know him. Philip was familiar with Jesus, yet there is a since in which that familiarity inhibited him from seeing Jesus *as the Father.*

There is a popular tendency to misunderstand Jesus' instruction in John 14 like Philip. Many of us suppose that Jesus' climactic declaration that "No one comes to the Father except through me" means "no one gets to heaven except through me." We then take our paraphrase to be the very *essence* of the gospel, depriving Jesus' message of its personal and practical implications. While his message of course includes a *future* life with the Father for those who are in him, it is also in Christ that we engage in intimate relationship with the Father *now.* If this sounds new (at best) or bizarre (at worst) to folks who have been Christian a long time, it is not because Jesus has been unclear. It is because we have not listened. We are familiar with his message, but we do not know him. Yet when we allow Jesus do deconstruct our familiarities, we will find ourselves engulfed in a life – a "Way" – which involves knowing God day by day in Christ *en route* to the Father.

Questions for Further Thinking

Read John 14 in its entirety. Pay careful attention to the way Jesus speaks of life with him, the

Father, and the coming Helper. Is this a passage which only pertains to future, heavenly events, or can you detect an actual *life* with the Trinity being offered?

Prayer

Father,
we thank you for your coming to us, that we may have a way into life with you:
Forgive us for our presumptions and [over]familiarity with Jesus' teaching and instruction; give us fresh eyes, ears, and hearts to hear from Jesus, that we may see him as more than merely a way to post-mortem paradise, but also as a way of life here on earth; and grant that we may enter into this life *now* and for all eternity;
through Jesus Christ, who is indeed the way, the truth, and the life, Amen.

JESUS IS NEARER THAN WE THINK
Revelation 3:20
Bohye Kim

"Very few people today find Jesus interesting as a person or of vital relevance to the course of their actual lives. He is not generally regarded as a real-life personality who deals with real-life issues but is thought to be concerned with some feathery realm other than the one we must deal with, and must deal with *now*. And frankly, he is not taken to be a person of much ability."
(*DC*, XII)

When you think about Jesus, what image does appears in your mind? My instant image of Jesus is a Mediterranean man with dark-olive-colored skin and curly short hair with a white long dress. Even though I grew up seeing numerous, vivid illustrations of western Jesus—a handsome-looking white man with blonde hair and a short mustache and beard—those images failed to create in me a notion that Jesus has a "real-life personality," in which I can actually relate myself to him in my "real-life." The image of Jesus in my mind was hanging on the wall in a frame, and actually not as a real personality whom I can deal with him *now*.

I began wondering why I felt so much distance to Jesus. Is it the images and ideas of Jesus that I picked up at Sunday school classes, which became a fossil in my mind? Or, could it be that I did not have the intention or desire to relate my "real-life" to Jesus? Or, did I just put Jesus in my own box and not think that about Jesus's "real-life personality?" In fact, Jesus tells us that he stands at the door, knocking: "Listen! I am standing at the door, knocking; if you hear my voice and open the door, I will come in to you and eat with you, and you with me" (Rev 3:20).

Jesus is knocking on the door. Jesus is ready to be relate with us. Jesus is prepared to come in to us and have communion with us. It is now our turn to hear this "real-life personality" Jesus knocking on our door. It is now time to realize that Jesus is willing to relate to us and to our "real-life." Let us be intentional about welcoming Jesus in to our "real-life," and let us enjoy being related to this "real-life personality" Jesus.

Questions for Further Thinking

What is it that makes us think Jesus is far away from our "*now*?" After realizing that Jesus is closer to your direct life and that he is with you *now,* how might this change your idea about Jesus? Can it affect the way you live your "*now*?"

How can we hear Jesus's voice and open the door to him in my "real-life?" How would that look like? How can I begin *now?*

Prayer

Loving God, you fully portrayed your love by sending your son into the world, and Jesus willingly demonstrated your love to us through his life: Remind us daily of your love shown in Jesus; and help us to realize that Jesus is real, standing at the door, and waiting for me to open my heart to him; in Jesus's name, Amen.

WHAT REALLY HAPPENED
Mark 8:22-25
Spencer Engelke

"Many in our day no longer have the ability to read the Bible or historic Christian events realistically, as if they really happened as described."
(DC, 80)

In history classes, textbooks, news, there is most commonly no interjection or skepticism on the belief that spoken events perspired. However, what is growing more and more frequent in our day and age is people reading the Bible and viewing it as a good story, rather than actual historical fact. This distortion can be quite detrimental to one's faith because when there is a notion of God's action not being the reality, there is a temptation to view God as not real. Meaning that the belief of God is there; however, there is not a belief that we are communing and living life with a God that is real and present in our world. This condition causes believers to rationalize God as being distanced or an idea, rather than a tangible Lord.

Jesus healing the blind man in Mark 8 gives a great example of what viewing God as neither historical or real can do to us. In this narrative, people bring a blind man to Jesus and ask to heal him (Mark 8:22). Jesus complies, and after spiting and laying his hands on the man's eyes he asks, "Do you see anything?" (Mark 8:23). The replies, "I see people; they look like trees walking around." After this Jesus puts his hands on the eyes again and the blind man sees clearly (Mark 8:24-25). You see, the first time the man saw, but his vision was blurry. This was an example of how people were viewing Jesus at that time. They did not understand who precisely Jesus was, but could make out enough to see his miracles and teachings, but not his person. If we as believers do not view God as historically accurate, we will not get the full picture on who God is. Thus, we will have a blurred vision of the Kingdom, the Heavens, and God. In order to honestly see clearly, we must view God as real in all facets of this world.

Questions for Further Thinking

Why do you think people do not view the Bible as historical fact? What causes them to write the Bible off as a story?

How can you see God clearly and not blurry as the man in the story? Are their things/disbeliefs in your life that cause distortion on your view of God?

Prayer

God the Father, the creator of the Heavens and the Earth,
thank you for your making yourself real to us daily; Thank you for your revelation in your Son, Christ:
help us to see you clearly and without distortion, to steadily walk with you throughout our days; you are a God that wants to be known, and for your children to come to complete knowledge of yourself; allow us to pursue that reality daily;
In the name of Jesus Christ, Amen.

"ALWAYS," IN FACT, MEANS ALWAYS
Matthew 6:11, 34
Andrew Barrett

"Today I have God, and *he* has the provisions. Tomorrow will be the same. So I simply ask today for what I need for today, or ask now for what I need now." (*DC*, 261)

I have a tendency to fall into vain repetition when reciting the Lord's Prayer, be it corporately or in private. In particular, while I may ask God to provide my daily bread, in my introspection I discover that I often doubt that God cares about my daily, "small," needs. He is too busy running the cosmos to care about providing me food or clothes. I suspect I speak for more people than myself.

Jesus of course knew both the reality of doubts like mine, and the blatant irony of them all. That we could live in a world where birds are well fed and the grass of the fields are beautifully adorned, and yet we think God has little time to spare for us, his children, is indicative of our lack of trust and faith. On the same page as the above excerpt, Willard describes how astonishing and painful it would be if our children did not trust us for daily provision. Such is the affect our mistrust has on God.

Jesus' announcement was (and *is*) that the kingdom of the heavens is here and accessible to all, meaning – in essence – that *God* is here and available to all. In his ever-presence he desires that we trust in his provision of our daily needs, because *he has them to offer*. All that is required on our part is to *ask* (Matt. 7.7). Exercised in this way, prayer frees us from concerns about the future, because we have the utmost confidence in God, our provider, who is present with us each day. We can cease worrying about tomorrow, because we know God will be with us tomorrow, providing for us in the same way he does today.

Questions for Further Thinking

Consider the *content* of your time(s) of prayer. Do you ask for God's provision in all things, or do you only call upon God's help for the "big stuff"?

What "daily bread" could you practice asking for God to on a daily basis? While it does not *have* to be food, consider a regular need that would make for good practice in trusting God for daily provision.

<u>Prayer</u>

Imminent God,
whose generosity spans from the Incarnation to our daily bread:
Grant us to know that you are concerned with our concerns; teach us to confide in you for the provision of things we consider small or unimportant; that our anxieties about the future may cease because of our certainty of your presence and provision;
through Jesus Christ our Lord. Amen.

JESUS IS INTERESTED IN ME
Isaiah 40:28
Bohye Kim

"... I am learning from Jesus how to lead my life, my whole life, my real life…And he is, in any case, interested in my life, that very existence that is me." (*DC*, 283)

As Christians, we know and remember that Jesus died *for* us at the cross. Crucifixion is the big event in Christianity. My question at this point is, how much time do we spend time meditating on the idea that Jesus acted out such love on the cross *for me*. How much emphasis do we put on the preposition "*for*" to realize Jesus's direct relation to me, "that very existence" of me? As I grew up in a Christian home, I heard the *story* of Jesus's life numerous times, at church and at home. Born in a manger, Jesus was a clever kid who taught the rabbis. Before his ministry began, he was a carpenter. Once the ministry began, he was a humble and brilliant leader who healed, taught, and prayed. And when it was time, after Jesus's last prayer on the mountain, Judas betrayed him, and Jesus's affliction began. He stood in front of the court. He got brutally beaten. He carried the heavy cross up to the hill. At Golgotha, Jesus hung on the cross. And in three days, he resurrected.

This is the *story* of Jesus, and my knowledge accepted it as Jesus's life *story* on the earth. However, my heart did not recognize the direct relation between such *story* and my story. John 3:16 clearly tells us that God sent his son because he loved the world dearly. When I cognitively assented to Jesus's *story* to affect my life, his *story* was not a mere account from a novel's storytelling. It was Jesus's attention. It was his interest in my life, in my being. I realized the familiarity that I had with Jesus's life *story*, which prevented me from interacting with Jesus's personality. I was limiting Jesus's love for me. Isaiah 40:28 clearly notes that God's "understanding is unsearchable," for he does not faint or grow weary. Jesus understands you. Jesus is interested in you because Jesus loves you.

Questions for Further Thinking

Do we consider Jesus as a mere protagonist of a story, rather than a real personality who is deeply interested in us?

How does Jesus's life story affect your story?

<u>Prayer</u>

Heavenly Father, you have sent your son into the world to express how much you are interested in our life and our being:
We praise you for your unsearchable understanding; forgive us for limiting your existence in our lives with our limited minds; remind us how much you are interested in us; and help us to form an actual relationship with Jesus, your son;
in His name, Amen.

EYES CLOSED
Luke 17:21
Spencer Engelke

"Nothing – no human being or institution, no time, no space, no spiritual being, no event stands between God and those who trust in him. The "heavens" are always there with you no matter what." (*DC*, 77)

I remember one time when my family gathered around the table to eat dinner. As we were about to eat my mom stated with sternness, "Close your eyes we are praying." I, being eight at the time, closed my eyes and listened to the prayer of my dad. However, losing focus, I opened my eyes and took a quick peek around the room. Turning my head, my sister's eyes and mine met, with a smug look in her face she proceeded to close her eyes. Immediately after the prayer, my sister yells, "Spencer's eyes were open!" My Dad turns to her and says, "How would you know if had your eyes closed?"

Maybe you can relate to that story. Closing one's eyes during prayer is a common practice for Christians. However, the question is, why do we close our eyes to eliminate the "distractions" of the world if God and the "heavens" are in the world around us? That is the same as removing an artist's painting because it distracts the audience from the artist. God's creation is the evidence and the masterwork of his good will and work (Job 12:7-10). Furthermore, God's presence and the "heavens" are in the midst of the atmosphere we are breathing and living (Luke 17:21). So, to view God's presence as only something believers conjure up in their minds is incomplete and lacking the fullness of the Kingdom.

The Kingdom of God is active and present in the lives of the believer. However, if the believers are not actively seeking the Kingdom, it can be missed. I would challenge you to seek God in everything, not just in action or creation but in the air we breathe. Believing God and the "heavens" are here presently, and we can enter into that truth.

Questions for Further Thinking

Have you ever actively sought the Kingdom of God in your daily life? How did/do you think that would affect your pursuit of God?

Do you think removing the Lord from the world is something that we as believers should do? Or do you believe that we should see God in creation?

Prayer

Oh God of heavens, the Holy One of Israel,
thank you for your creation and our ability to see you through your majestic work:
Help us to view you as in and amongst us and not separated by a vast chasm; your creation is a testament to your love, joy, beauty, and purpose; allow us to see you more clearly in that.
In the name of Jesus Christ, Amen.

THE MINIMUM REQUIREMENT
Mark 9:14-29
Andrew Barrett

"Jesus' disciples are those who have chosen to be with him to learn to be like him. All they have necessarily realized at the outset of their apprenticeship to him is, *Jesus is right.*" (*DC,* 318)

The sort of life with God we are learning about from Willard in this little book might seem to many to be for the extra-spiritual or the well-learned. We suppose that if we *just* reach a certain level of doctrinal proficiency of spiritual discernment that we will then be able to live the life with God that Jesus offers, and yet the present passage contends that it is quite the opposite.

The father of the demon-possessed boy has not come to terms with the comprehensive scope of Jesus' ministry. He has no preferred theory of atonement, and is not a consistent practitioner of the spiritual disciples. He is a man whose son is in grave danger, and he believes Jesus can do something about it. In regards to the stuff he has not quite come to terms with, he desperately (and honestly) pleas "Help my unbelief" (9.24). In response to this petition Jesus acts, almost as if to say "That is quite alright, we'll start from here," and he heals the boy, indicating to the father that if his ailed boy can be entrusted to Jesus, so can his entire life.

Willard later argues that in response to our initial captivation by Jesus, "He then leads us to genuine understanding and reliance upon God in every aspect of our life. But that progression takes some time."[1] The life of intimate relationship with God does not happen quickly, and is not reserved for the spectacular. To the contrary, it is reserved for those who meet the minimum requirement: belief in Jesus' rightness, and from there proceed into a life of discipleship to the Teacher. Christ will indeed sort out our unbelief, but that happens as the journey goes on. Not before it.

Questions for Further Thinking

Have you tended to think that "discipleship" or "life with God" was reserved for "special" Christians (ministers, theologians, monks, etc.)?

---

[1] *DC,* 319.

Recall the time you decided to follow Jesus. What about Christ inspired you to give your life to him, and what elements of your life might cause to share the father's request of "Help my unbelief"?

<u>Prayer</u>

Father,
we are humbled by your gentleness and patience toward us:
Meet us at our point of greatest need; teach us that just as you tend to the needs we trust you can do something about, so you will tend to those needs and desires we are uncertain of; give us a spirit of willingness to embark on the long journey of life with you; and walk along with us, graciously picking us up as we stumble; we believe, Lord, help our unbelief;
Amen.

DEPENDING ON JESUS
Colossians 3:15
Bohye Kim

"We are only thinking about how to become one [disciple]. Nevertheless, we can count on Jesus to meet us in our admittedly imperfect efforts to put his word into practice. Where his word is, there he is. He does not leave his words to stand along in the world. And his loveliness and strength will certainly be personally revealed to those who will simply make the effort do what his words indicate." (*DC*, 296)

This is often how we think: We are Christians. As Christians, we should go to church every Sunday. We should tithe. We should attend Sunday school classes to gain knowledge about the one whom we believe in. We should spend a certain amount of time every day on a personal devotional time. We should love our neighbors. We should forgive our enemies. We should do this, and we should that.

Have you ever been overwhelmed or panicked by your own limited efforts to be a follower of Jesus? We often find a long list of things that we "should be doing" as Christians. Are we cognitively pushing ourselves to be disciples of Jesus by our own strength and knowledge? Do we tend to associate *thinking about* these things as *practicing* them? As Dallas Willard mentions above in the quote, we tend to think and worry about becoming a disciple of Jesus and forget about practicing to become one.

Once we realize that following Jesus is not about how much effort we put in, we find peace in the fact that as we walk with Jesus everyday and depend on his strength, he willfully supports us. As Willard reminds us, we can depend on Jesus's "loveliness and strength" to personally help us become disciples of him. Not by our own strength or expectation as Christians, but by Jesus' loving support in his words for us. Let us decide to be disciples of Jesus, and let us fully depend upon our teacher's strength, joy, and loveliness instead of our own limited strength.

Questions for Further Thinking

Did you ever depend upon your own strengths to think on how to become a disciple of Jesus?
If yes, in what aspect did it help you to successfully to become a disciple of Jesus? If no, what did it do to you?

How can we practice to have willingness to be a disciple of Jesus and depend upon his strength?

Prayer

Loving Jesus, you have loved us so much that you did not stop loving us even today:
Your love supports us every day, and your peace rules our hearts; we thank you for your beautiful and active love that knows not to support us; help us to depend upon your strength and your loveliness;
in Jesus's name, Amen.

ACCESS VS. EXISTENCE
Matthew 7
Spencer Engelke

"Jesus' own gospel of the kingdom was not that the kingdom was about to come, or had recently come, into existence. If we attend to what he actually said, it becomes clear that his gospel concerned only the new accessibility of the kingdom to humanity through himself." (*DC,* 34)

Far too often people read Jesus' proclamation that the kingdom of heaven is here (Matt. 5-7) as an invitation, not a statement of fact. The kingdom of heaven always existed and is seen throughout Old Testament (Isa. 52:7, Exod. 15:18, Ps. 96). So, why is it popular belief that the kingdom of heaven arrived when Jesus arrived? To answer this question, we first have to decide what the kingdom of heaven is and what the kingdom of heaven is not.

The kingdom of heaven is not a social or political reality. If the kingdom was a political or social entity, then it would be limited to the one reality. However, as we see in the Lord's prayer that God's will be done on "earth as in heaven" (Luke 11:2), God's kingdom is both in heaven and on earth and cannot be limited to one reality. In the same light the kingdom of heaven is not isolated in the "in the hearts of men" (Luke 17:21). Yes, the kingdom is in the hearts of men but in the same manner as the political reality, the kingdom cannot be limited.

The kingdom of heaven is simply God's own will, where what God wants is done (*DC,* 33). So, the effect of Jesus' proclamation is not announcing that the kingdom of heaven has come into existence, rather Jesus is announcing a new accessibility to the kingdom through himself. What that means for us today is that when pray about the kingdom we are not asking God to bring something into existence but giving God permission to infuriate the parts of our lives that are not in God's direct rule.

Questions for Further Thinking

Before the reading how do you interpret Jesus' proclamation "the kingdom of heaven is at hand"? What has changed since this reading?

How can you in your daily life allow the kingdom of heaven to be at hand?

<u>Prayer</u>

Our Heavenly Father,
we praise you for your great name. A name that is above every other name. A name that has the power to save, a power cause even the greatest of evil to cripple at the sound:
We petition for you to take over every point of our lives to be under your perfect and loving demonian; allow us to follow you and enter into your presence and kingdom every single moment; In the name of Jesus Christ. Amen.

MAKING THE TREE GOOD
2 Corinthians 5:12
Andrew Barrett

"They key in such cases is to aim at the heart and its transformation. We want to "make the tree good." We do not aim *just* to control behavior, but to change the inner castle of the soul, that God may be worshipped "in spirit and in truth" and right behavior cease to be a performance."
(*DC,* 364)

Paul knew affliction. The scope of his hardship was so broad that he was able to provide three separate lists of them in 2 Corinthians (3:8-9; 6:4-10; 11:16-29). Despite the destruction of Paul's outer self, he is sure that "we have wronged no one, corrupted no one, we have taken advantage of no one" (7.2) and he entreats the Corinthians to grasp the reality of his apostleship so that they may resist those who over-value outward appearances (5.12). Paul's opponents thought that outward appearances were the essence of life with God. Yet Paul understood that right behavior divorced from kingdom-hearts were dead works. Works that, in the long run, cannot be sustained, because they are not indicative to the *true* character of the doer.

Many of us understand that the life with God which we are invited to involves a change of behavior. The problem is not in our sense that we should be behaving in a certain way, but in thinking that if we would *just* sort our behavior out, the heart will soon follow suit. Jesus, Paul, and Dallas Willard see that as backwards, teaching instead that the heart is where whatever is commendable or condemnable resides.

Perhaps we try to jump straight to behavioral correction because we are impatient. We do not wish to learn and be formed. We cannot simply dress up the fruit we bear, because even the best of cosmetic work cannot hide a foul tree. The goal is to make the tree *good*. To fix our desires on God in such a way that abhorring and resisting evil becomes second nature. This does not involve living by a certain set of rules. It involves walking with Jesus along the way, being taught and formed by him so that our very *lives* are transformed.

Questions for Further Thinking

Have you tried to work yourself into the kind of person you sense Jesus calling you to be?

In what ways do we continue to put a premium on outward appearances? How does this hinder our life in the kingdom of God?

Prayer

Almighty God,
who is at work renewing our inner self day by day as we step into life we you:
Forgive us for our lingering attempts at works righteousness; teach us to confide in you for growth and spiritual direction; that we may be formed into good trees which bear delicious fruit without a second thought;
in Jesus' name, Amen.

WALKING IN JESUS
Colossians 2:6-7
Bohye Kim

"True Christlikeness, true companionship with Christ, comes at the point where it is hard not to respond as he would." (*SD*, 8)

Colossians 2:6-7 tells us, "As you therefore have received Christ Jesus the Lord, continue to live your lives in him, rooted and built up in him and established in the faith, just as you were taught, abounding in thanksgiving." We know that we should walk *in* Jesus once we receive him as our Lord and Savior. But what exactly is living *in* Jesus and walking *in* him?

I heard such concept about walking with Jesus through both Christian contemporary music and hymns. I learned in Sunday school class about it since I was a kindergartener. Naturally, I accepted the act of walking in Jesus as a part of my life, without *truly* knowing, *truly* experiencing it, and *truly* being changed to be like him. I always had a question: How does walking *in* Jesus look like? Is it putting my effort in loving my enemies, turning the other cheek, going an extra mile, and suffering patiently? What if I get tired of following Jesus because it is just too difficult and neither joyful or fun? What if I don't want to follow Jesus for a moment or a day because other things are more enjoyable than following Jesus? Dallas Willard has clearly pointed out my symptom. I devoutly believed in the "power of effort-at-the-moment-of-action" to accomplish what I wanted and totally disregarded the "need for character change" in my life as a whole.[2].

I have been trying to follow Jesus because I knew I *had to*, not because I *wanted to*. Instead of accepting Jesus' overall way of life as my way of life, I simply customized a set of goals of my own "To be like Jesus Project." Instead of spending time with my loving Savior and learning from him directly, I stood in distance from Jesus, considered the Bible as a textbook or a cookbook, and tried to act exactly what the book told me to. My heart was not attracted. Instead of walking *in* Jesus, I walked by

---

[2] *SD*, 8.

myself, feeling that Jesus was at distance. I had no interaction with him. There was no joy in my "To be like Jesus Project."

Walking in Jesus is not boring. It is a joyful life. It is not so complicated that you have to measure every act of yours and judge on your own. Rather, it is a holistic change of your character that, with the result that "it is hard not to respond as he [Jesus] would."[3]

Questions for Further Thinking

What is your "To be like Jesus Project"?

What was your definition of walking in Jesus before reading this devotion, and what is your understanding of walking in Jesus after reading Dallas Willard's quote above?

Prayer

Almighty Jesus,
you have been waiting for us to walk in you when we tried to walk by ourselves:
We thank you for calling us and waiting for us to walk in you; give us your loving courage and deep joy as our characters change like yours;
through Jesus Christ our Lord, Amen.

---

[3] *SD*, 8.

IS LAUGHTER THE BEST MEDICINE?
Psalm 126:1-2
Spencer Engelke

"He was a master of humor and often used it to drive home the truths he imparted, as any good speaker does. But few today would put him on their guest list for a party – if it were really going to be a party. Just as we don't think of Jesus as intelligent, so we don't think of him as pleasant company, someone to enjoy being around." (*DC,* 262)

We have all heard the phrase, "laughter is the best medicine." That is not scientifically true, because antibiotics do vastly more healing for an infection than laughter. However, there is some merit to that statement. Whenever you are having fun and being with people you love, laughter almost inevitably follows. Laughter is like the physical manifestation of a good time. So, why do we dissociate laughter and joy with being in the presence of the Lord? Reverence is a vital and essential component to the faith, but if we become people that do not love the Lord's presence then are we God's people? What child does not desire to have fun with his/her father?

This joy is the intent behind the words of Psalm 126:2 "Our mouths were filled with laughter, our tongues with songs of joy, Then it was said among the nations, 'The Lord has done great things for them.'" This a song of praise after the Lord restored Zion. There is an immense amount of joy in the words of the people writing this song. However, do we get that kind of language, that joy, in our Christian walk today?

God wants to be a God of joy and laughter and has proven to be that. If we as believer distance ourselves from understanding God in that way, we do ourselves a disservice. So many things on this earth are enticing and fun, why shouldn't the Creator of those things be just as, or if not more, enticing and fun? Walking in joy and laughter is contagious and highly sought after, if we can pursue the Lord in that light, our walk will become much more alive.

Questions for Further Thinking

Have you ever thought about God laughing? How does God having a sense of humor change your image of God?

How can we walk in laughter and joy with God? What are some steps we can take to make that practice a reality?

Prayer

Lord, God of the universe,
thank you for your sense of humor:
Thank you for imparting and for giving us the gift of laughter; we know all good things come from you and cannot help but praise you for them; help us to view you as a God of joy and happiness; a God that would be the life of the party; your joyfulness is a testament to your character and your desire for your children to be joyful; let us live into that jubilance you call us to;
In the name of Jesus Christ, Amen.

COOPERATIVE SPIRITUALITY
John 20:21-22
Andrew Barrett

"A 'spiritual life' consists in that range of activities in which people cooperatively interact with God – and with the spiritual order deriving from God's personality and God's action." (*SD*, 67)

How have we tended to define "spirituality"? I would imagine that – if that is even a word we are comfortable using – we might assign the word a broad definition like "my relationship with God." While that is not a definition I would dispute, our text invites us to view "spirituality" afresh.

Having risen from the grave, Jesus offers his disciples a powerful commission. "As the Father has sent me," says Jesus, "even so I am sending you" (20:21). Recall that in John's Gospel Jesus is the Word made flesh (1:14) who is written of as being in *total cooperation* with his Father who sent him. Now, with his ascension in the near future, *Jesus commissions his disciples to share in that same cooperation.* John then writes that Jesus "breathed on them," saying, "receive the Holy Spirit" (20:22), echoing God's life-giving breath given to Adam in Genesis 2.

From the very beginning, God has desired humanity to cooperate with him as those who are integrated into and dominated by his kingdom.[4] Now, in Christ, the invitation is renewed. God invites us to cooperate with him, not as equal partners, but as his beloved children. This is quite like when a father asks his child to join him in, say, tending the garden. There is no question that the father is capable of finishing the job himself (indeed, it would probably be easier *without* the help of the child), and yet the father so loves his child that he delights in his help, however insufficient. The child will develop skill(s) over time. What matters most is the time spent working together. Such is the case for spirituality.

Questions for Further Thinking

---

[4] *SD*, 67.

What are your initial reactions to Willard's idea that spirituality is cooperating with God?

We often can describe what we are saved *from*, but how does our reading – both from Willard and from Scripture – help us understand what we are saved *for*?

Prayer

Father,
who graciously invites us to take part in the work you are doing:
Forgive us for the multitude of times we have refused your invitation; we, like spoiled children, so often opt to remain inside doing our own thing rather than joining you out in the world; help us to respond in love to your call; teach us to marvel at your mindfulness of humanity;
through Christ our Lord, Amen.

RETURNING TO JESUS WITH ALL MY HEART
Joel 2:12
Bohye Kim

"How can Jesus be my Lord if I don't even *plan* to obey him?" (*SD*, 13)

In the first half of Joel 2:12, the Lord summons the reader to turn to him with all our hearts: "Yet even now, says the LORD, return to me with all your heart, with fasting, with weeping, and with mourning." Have you ever had a moment where believing in Jesus Christ felt like a repetitive ritual that lacked any kind of vibrancy, joy, and liveliness? Have you ever had a moment where you did not even think about obeying him and his words because you forgot to obey? Or, did his command to give our heart to him become a nebulous idea, instead of being reality? Did you ever wonder what he wanted in from you? According to Joel 2:12, the Lord wants our heart.

Growing up in a Christian home, I mentally assented to the fact that I needed to have some kind of relationship with Jesus. I *knew* that I needed to talk to him for a certain amount of time every day in prayer. I *knew* that reading the Bible was essential in figuring out what Jesus wanted from me. As I reflect on my young Christian life, I recall making a long "to-do-list" on how to become a good follower of Jesus. The list became a ritual to me, which lacked my heart. There was practice, but not my heart. There was ritual, which lacked vibrancy and joy. I did not *plan* to give my heart to Jesus. Instead of *planning* how to give my heart to him, practicing it, and making such obedience realistic in my life, it was all about cognitive exercise—knowing what I *should* be doing.

If we *plan* to obey Jesus, we are *planning* to return to him with all of our hearts. We are deciding to give our hearts to Jesus, instead of giving it to someone or something else that is not of him. Instead of merely doing rituals to be considered as good Christians, how about *planning* to give our hearts to Jesus?

Questions for Further Thinking

How does your personal devotional time look like? Are you doing it to be considered as a good Christian, or are you doing it to give your heart to Jesus?

What is your *plan* in obeying Jesus?

Prayer

Heavenly Father,
you have been waiting for us to give our hearts to you:
We thank you for demonstrating your love through your Son, Jesus Christ, so that we can learn how to love you by giving our hearts to you; remind us daily that you are waiting and wanting our hearts; encourage us to *plan* to give our hearts to you;
through Jesus Christ our Lord, Amen.

LITERAL RATHER THAN FIGURATIVE
Mark 12:41-44
Spencer Engelke

"The context of the Kingdom Among Us transforms the respective actions. "Little is much," we say, "When God is in it." And so it is. Really."
(DC, 101)

Jesus's teachings transform and morph our reality from a strictly physical, to a unified mixture of the spiritual and physical world. In most cases, Jesus's pronouncements do not make physical sense. For example, the famous passage, "Whoever finds his life will lose it, and whoever loses his life for my sake will find it." (Matthew 10:39), does not make sense analytically. How can a person gain, find, and keep something if they chose to lose it? This question gets to the heart of Jesus's words because the temptation is to view his words and sayings as figurative, disallowing the immense potential they garner to impact on our lives. However, if we begin to believe Jesus's word and have our reality shaped by the Creator, these words to start to develop us into Christ's image.

One of the best examples of this idea is found in Jesus's proclamation of the widows offering. In this section in Mark's Gospel, Jesus is standing near the front of the temple watching people tithe. He begins to see many rich people put large sums of money into the box, then a poor widow walks up to the box and places two small copper coins. Jesus, seeing the poor widow's offering, calls his disciples and tells them that this woman gave more than all of the rich people (Mark 12:41-44). Again, this does not make sense on a physical level, mathematically large sums of money are more than two small copper coins. However, as we allow Jesus's words to shape our reality, we see what God can do with our actions and that God creates the relative value, therefore, the little with God is much greater than an abundance without God.

Questions for Further Thinking

Have you ever thought of what dictates and morphs your reality? How can we allow God, not our social context, to shape our understanding and rational?

How do we take Jesus's teaching literally? Can you think of an example in your life where you did what Jesus literally commanded?

Prayer

Father God,
the creator of the heaven and the earth:
Thank you for your constant gift of wisdom; thank you for allowing us the ability for our worldview to be shaped by you alone; praise your great name for all the provisions and grace you lavish on us every single day; please continue to form and mold us into the image of your son, in our mind, body, and spirit; Lord allow your thoughts and your actions be ours; your goodness and care are all a testament to your love for us; we implore you to manifest yourself more in our lives;
In the name of Jesus Christ, Amen

SHARED GLORY
Psalm 8
Andrew Barrett

"I believe men and women were designed by God, in the very constitution of their human personalities, to carry out his rule by meshing the relatively little power resident in their own bodies with the power inherent in the infinite Rule or Kingdom of God." (*SD*, 54)

In a previous devotion I treated Willard's definition of "spirituality" as cooperating with God in conversation with Jesus' words in John 20:21-22. What we have in our present quote and passage is an important brick to lay on that foundation: that God wishes to share the glory he receives as we live in cooperation with him *with us*.

Consider the words of Psalm 8. This psalm is, of course, a Christological one – anticipating the glory of God's Messiah. It would be wrong, however, to let the buck stop there, for what we discover as we meditate on the passage is that the psalm speaks to our very own existence. God in his loving generosity has given us dominion over the works of *his* hands (8:6), and in so doing has crowned *us* with glory and honor (8:5). Willard calls this humanity's "original job description,"[5] and now in Christ we are reenrolled on the payroll.

Building on a previous illustration, the father not only invites us to join in on what he is up to, but teaches us, equipping us to embark on our own projects in such a way that it is *evident* that we have learned from the best. We combine our expertise – though the father's is far superior – and through ongoing relationship and work we emerge as those equipped for doing the work as the father himself would, no longer requiring their direct supervision and intervention. Something like that, I think, is how God relates to us. He alone is the Lord whose name is majestic over all the earth; he alone has set his glory above the heavens; and yet he is mindful of *us,* crowning *us* with glory and honor as beloved children.

Questions for Further Thinking

---

[5] *SD*, 54

If Psalm 8 is *indeed* about us, what implications does that have for our manner of living?

Prayer

Father,
who not only invites us to work alongside you, but desires to share your glory with us:
We rejoice that you, the creator of heaven and earth, would be mindful of us in such a way as to place the works of your hands under our feet; may the joy of such consideration compel us to good works; may we, as those in Christ, share in the life of Christ as your beloved children, such that we see ourselves and our work as of the importance that you see them; in Jesus' name, Amen.

DAILY NEWNESS
Ezekiel 36:26
Bohye Kim

"Why is it that we look upon our salvation as a moment that began our religious life instead of the daily life we receive from God?" (*SD*, 28)

When you first hear the word *salvation,* what comes into your mind? Before reading Dallas Willard's perspective on salvation, I understood it to be a concept which determined my ultimate destination after the physical life. I knew salvation was the crucial aspect in Christianity. I learned that Jesus opened the way to our individual salvation through his ministry on earth. I was told that Jesus is the only one who can provide salvation. In other words, I intellectually understood the importance of salvation, but that was it. My thought process stopped at the point of realization of its importance. I did not think about asking, "So what? How does such knowledge impact my everyday life?"

As Dallas Willard inquires, why do we tend to think of salvation as an important matter that happens *not now* but at one point in our religious life? Why is it *then* and not *now*? God tells us in Ezekiel 36:26 that he will give us a new heart: "A new heart I will give you, and a new spirit I will put within you; and I will remove from your body the heart of stone and give you a heart of flesh." If we think about salvation in the way Dallas Willard inquires us, we receive salvation every day. The sense of it is renewed within us, which affects our thinking, emotions, actions, the way we see daily incidences, and the way we interact with God. Daily newness of the notion of salvation humbles our attitude toward God and our neighbors. It creates in us joy and gratitude. It protects our minds from distractions of the world. Let us begin thinking about salvation as a daily gift from God, and let our heart be renewed.

Questions for Further Thinking

Why do you think there is a sense of distance when we "look upon salvation"?

What makes us think that salvation is not "the daily life we receive from God"?

Prayer

Glorious Father,
you have given us the gift of salvation through your only begotten Son, Jesus Christ:
We thank you for the gift and reminding us that the gift is given to us not at one point but every day; humble us to receive your gift of salvation with joy and gratitude;
in Jesus' name, Amen.

PRAYING IN PRIVACY
Matthew 6:5-8
Spencer Engelke

"So when the children of the kingdom pray, they may even disappear from sight for they have learned to be indifferent to whether other know of their prayer or not. They enter a private room and close the door."
(DC, 213)

Prayer is an enigma in today's society. There are a vast number of books, articles, thoughts, etc. about prayer. It seems as if prayer is this elusive practice that one must perfect to indeed participate in it. People even seem somewhat shy and embarrassed when asked to pray in front of people because they do not want to run of the risk of sounding "bad." However, Jesus teaches us that we are to communicate to the Father through prayer and if prayer is our primary communication line we should take full advantage of the opportunity. We should not be fearful or prideful of how we sound or the thoughts of others, on the contrary, we should seek opportunities to be alone with God.

Matthew 6:5-8 encourages believers to pray with intentionality and in secret so that our Father will reward us. The Pharisees had the practice of standing in the synagogues and street corners bloviating these highly articulate and beautiful prayers to impress and suppress the people around them (Matt. 6:5). Jesus claims that they have their reward by the social status gained through these prayers. Though, to be rewarded in secret, Jesus's claims is far better. That is because when one talks to the Father alone, they can have a one on one conversation with God. Here is a practical example: If a person is communicating to another friend in a group setting the intentionality and deepness of that conversation can only be taken so far, due to the distractions of the situation. However, if a person can sit down with that friend and have a one on one conversation, the limits placed on the intentionality due to the group setting disappear. The person can begin to know and build a relationship with the friend honestly. In the same manner, when we have one on one conversations with God, we can know the Lord more and establish a much more profound relationship with the God of the universe.

Questions for Further Thinking

Why can prayer be so intimidating? Why do we feel so compelled to say a "good" prayer?

Do you view prayer as a one on one conversation with God? How can praying in secret be more beneficial than praying for social status?

Prayer

God Almighty,
the fortress for the weak and the home for the homeless:
Thank you for your constant gift of prayer; thank you for allowing us the ability to have a one on one conversation with you and you alone; praise you for your mercies are new each day and your grace is sufficient in our weakness; please convict us to find a place to be alone with you and pray; Lord, reward us in secret and hear our prayers;
in the name of Jesus Christ, Amen.

SAVED AND BEING SAVED
1 Corinthians 1:18
Andrew Barrett

"…it is necessary to say that conversion, as understood in Christian circles, is *not* the same thing as *the required transformation of the self.* The fact that a long course of experience is needed for the transformation is not set aside when we are touched by the new life from above" (*SD,* 70)

We have spoken a great deal of the intimate relationship God desires to have with us, and the transformation, work, and glory that awaits those who accept the invitation. What Willard hurries to warn us of, though, is that transforming out of our sinful human condition takes time, such that it is dangerous to suppose the moment of conversion is the moment when the *whole* transformation occurs.

Indeed, in the selected passage the Apostle Paul uses language of "*being* saved." We may ask "I thought I was saved?" and of course that is true, too. Elsewhere Paul uses past-tense language to refer to our salvation (cf. 1 Cor. 6:11). This is not a contradiction, but a healthy tension. We are saved, and we are being saved. My title is a play on the Reformation expression *semper reformanda,* that is "always reformed/being reformed," reminding Protestants that the fresh reading of Scripture which catalyzed the Reformation was not a one-off affair, but one which was to be built upon by the Church through generations. Such is the case for our salvation: We are *saved.* Our salvation is not at risk. What *is* at risk, however, is our maturity into the kind of people who live as God always intended.

There are a number of disciplines that may be undertaken to achieve such maturity, but what is required first is to recognize that *Christians are to mature in Christ.* Think yet again to the father-in-the garden illustration. The child does not know the intricacies of gardening upon accepting the first invitation. Time and practice must be put in, with the hope that the child will mature into one who does no longer requires constant direct instruction, but who harmoniously works alongside their father.

Questions for Further Thinking

Read Philippians 2:12. How does Paul's instruction to work out our salvation influence our understanding of the topic?

Prayer

Father,
who welcomes us to participate in his wonderful work;
Help us to see that you are calling us into a *life*; comfort us, so that we may see maturing in Christ as a wonderful necessity; help us to see our spiritual growth as an opportunity to know you deeper and deeper;
in Jesus' name, Amen.

OUR CAPACITY TO INTERACT
2 Samuel 7:22
Bohye Kim

"…people are transformed by contact with God. In creation the human organism was endowed with astonishing capacities to interact—through individual, social, and historical development—with the realities around it, including the spiritual." (*SD*, 65-66)

Thinking in terms of spiritual discipline, what is the final goal of our spirituality? Isn't it developing intentionality in our interaction with God, and gradually letting such relationship transform our reality? One way to view the focal point of spiritual discipline is to realize the capacity we have to be in "contact with God."[6] At times, we give up on striving to relate to God daily because of our tendency to categorize spirituality into a feathery, nontangible realm. We therefore do not have the capacity to interact with him. However, because we are created with the capacity to interact within several aspects in the realm of life, Willard explains that we have enough capacity to interact "the spiritual."[7]

Have you ever wondered or put yourself in a dilemma regarding to your capacity to interact with God? This is a thought that I struggled with. Through my amateur understanding of spiritual discipline, I endeavored (without the type of knowledge that Willard underlines above) to have an interaction with God. Not seeing an instant change in my life left me thinking that I lacked the *capacity* to interact with God because the spiritual realm to was just too difficult to understand. However, Willard tells us that we have the capacity to interact the spiritual, and when we have contact with God, we can be transformed. Our thoughts can be transformed to the state where we realize the capacity to interact with our true Father. The erred point that I found in my own spiritual discipline was that I practiced it without being in *contact with* God. I lacked intentionality in the daily interaction with him. This act of consciousness and desire to *be* in contact with God is the point that I have missed.

---

[6] *SD*, 65.
[7] *SD*, 66.

Afterwards, knowing that I have the capacity to interact with God, being in contact with him was less complicated than I imagined. I imitated David's prayer in 2 Samuel 7:22, and began to talk to God to be in contact with him: "Therefore you are great, O Lord God; for there is no one like you, and there is no God besides you, according to all that we have heard with our ears."

We have the capacity to interact with the spiritual. Let us be in contact with God and know the capacity that God gave us to interact with him, and let us enjoy such interaction!

<u>Questions for Further Thinking</u>

What are your ways to be in contact with God?

What are some aspects that hinder the way you think about your capacity to interact with God?

<u>Prayer</u>

Heavenly Father,
you created us to have the capacity to interact with you:
We thank you for allowing us to realize that having an interaction with you can be real; remind our mind and heart to comprehend and experience that the interaction with you is the reality;
through Jesus Christ our Lord, Amen.

TRUE SPIRITUALITY
Philippians 2:12
Spencer Engelke

"Because just as with the physical, there is a specific round of activities we must do to establish, maintain, and enhance our spiritual powers. One must train as well as try."
(*SD*, 98)

How do athletes become the greatest in their sport? Is it just based on God-given talent, or is there something else needed? Any reasonable person would say, "No it is not just talent, hard work is necessary to be great." If that is obvious in the world of sports, or any other profession for that matter, why do we not have the same comprehension of spirituality? Does it not make sense that for one to be more become more spiritual, it takes hard work? Now I am not talking about our justification as believers being predicated on our hard work, that is our free gift from the Lord (Rom. 6:23). No, I am speaking about our spiritual growth and maturity that comes from pursuing the Lord. Paul exhorts the Philippians to "work out your own salvation with fear and trembling," (Phil. 2:12). Now Paul is not talking about their salvation in terms of justification, our redemption into a right relationship with God, but our *sanctification*, the process of becoming more like God.

We are called as believers to follow Christ and be transformed into the image of Christ (2 Cor. 3:18). Thus, it takes an active, not passive, effort to begin to train ourselves in godliness. Now, if we know that to further one's skills training and disciplining are required, we must start to have the mindset that to possess and enhance our spiritual skills, spiritual practice is needed. If we want a deeper and more fulfilling relationship with our Creator, does it not make sense that we must realign and pursue that relationship through hard work? Not that we are trying to earn any favor or grace, but we want to experience the Lord in more profound and more impactful ways. Thus, we sacrifice our time, effort, and desires to equip ourselves for the work of the Spirit better.

Questions for Further Thinking

Do you believe that to develop our spiritual ability further we must train ourselves in righteousness? Why does that seem like a heretical foreign concept to some?

How have you been pursuing your relationship with God? Are their practices in your life that are training you in the Spirit?

Prayer

God our Father,
thank you for your grace and love that we have the ability to experience every day:
Help us to see you more clearly and work out our salvation; you have given us the ability to work hard for your Kingdom and participate in your redemptive work; we pray that we never take for granted your atonement and your presence; give us the ability to know and understand you more; in the name of Jesus Christ, Amen.

CAREFUL CONSIDERATION
1 Corinthians 1:26-31
Andrew Barrett

"Yet [the world of the New Testament] is a world and a life that ordinary people have entered and are entering now. It is a world that seems open to us and beckons us to enter. We feel its call." (*RH*, 9)

Imagine being the recipients of 1 Corinthians. Reviewing the gospel as he first told it to them, Paul speaks of the incomprehensible power of the cross. In a way that is scandalous to some and ridiculous to others, God has exercised his power and wisdom through Christ crucified. God's foolishness, says Paul, is wiser than the wisest of men; his weakness stronger than all of their strength. "Need an example" suggests Paul, "consider your own calling" (cf. 1 Cor. 1:26a).

What Willard compels us to realize is that this glorious world of Scripture, this life of God in which the Corinthians are instrumental in God's efforts to "shame the wise," to "shame the strong," to "bring to nothing things that are" is one in which we too – ordinary as we may be – are invited, indeed *called*, to enter in. "Not many of you were wise according to worldly standards," says Paul (1.26b). Not many of us are on anyone's V.I.P list. We are not in the president's cabinet. We are – for the most part – extraordinarily ordinary. The comfort offered here by Paul and by Willard is that it is *in* our ordinariness that God calls us in Christ to be the means by which he is calling the world to account!

Willard is right to call the world of Scripture one which appears altogether different than the one in which we sense we are living. This world, however, is the *true* world, and God calls us to join the ranks of the host of ordinary folk he has used to advance his kingdom within it. The promises of this world are ours as they were theirs, for God is a generous God, and loves to share with his children.

Questions for Further Thinking

Read the assigned passage. How have you traditionally understood Paul's words here?

How does Willard challenge us to read passages of such promise?

<u>Prayer</u>

Father,
who delights in ordinary people;
We thank you that though the kingdoms of the world overlook us, you
see us, and call us into relationship with you; we are awed by your
impression of us, that we would be the ones though whom you shame the
wise and the strong; please, God, open our hearts to your call;
in Jesus' name, Amen.

ONLY GOD KNOWS MY DEPTH
Psalm 139:1-4
Bohye Kim

"We usually know very little about the things that move in our own soul, the deepest level of our life, or what is driving it…Only God knows our depths, who we are, and what we would do." (*RH*, 17)

David the psalmist proclaims how God knows us completely in Psalm 139:1-4. Let us join in to David's acknowledgement of God's omniscience for a second: "O Lord, you have searched me and known me. You know when I sit down and when I rise up; you discern my thought from far away. You search out my path and my lying down, and are acquainted with all my ways. Even before a word is on my tongue, O Lord, you know it completely." God knows our thoughts. He knows our intentions. He knows our hearts. He knows "our depths."[8] He knows what we are going to say with our mouths. It is not the knowing of ourselves that leads our lives. It is not our own wisdom that drives our lives. It is God's knowing of "our depths" that matters. Even though we say we know ourselves, in reality, we have no idea about the "deepest level of life," as Dallas Willard underlines in the quote above.

This simple message—*God knows our hearts*—which we heard and continue to hear over and over again in our Christian circles is the reality happening now and not a mere knowledge that happened long time ago. A problem that occurs between this message and us is the fact that we consider it as a hackneyed knowledge instead fresh reality, due to its lethargic redundancy. We hear about it over and over again without any staccatos or emphasis on the realness of it. At the end, we are going to stand in front of God, who knows us better than we do. We are not going to stand in front of a mirror and discern ourselves. We are not going to stand in front of people who have commented about us. It is God whom we are going to stand at the end. Only God can know "our depths." This simple message is more serious than we think.

Questions for Further Thinking

---

[8] *RH*, 17.

What were your reactions to Psalm 139:1-4? Was it realistic to you? If yes, how? If not, why?

What are some prejudices that hinder our minds to think that the psalmist's proclamation in Psalms 139 is a mere message that has no direct relation to us?

Prayer

God almighty,
you are my father who knows me very well:
I thank you for your omniscience, and I thank you for being my father;
help me to realize that it is you who knows the entirety of my being;
grant me wisdom to be aware that you know me and love me;
in Jesus' name, Amen.

SPIRITUALLY REDEFINED
1 Corinthians 15:56-57
Spencer Engelke

"Spirituality is simply the holistic quality of human life as it was meant to be, at the center of which is our relation to God." (*SD*, 77)

In today's culture and society, the term "spirituality" has many different interpretations. Some people conjure up this picture of freedom and being one with nature as spirituality; others view spirituality as a life apart from the physical. In light of the many ideas and thoughts about what spirituality is, we must ask: which one is the truth? That is the question we as believers must answer because, to grow spiritually, it is necessary to define spirituality. In the quote above, Willard defines spirituality as permanently living the life we were designed to inherit. Namely, an experience of living that God is at the center of. Everything we do, say, and think is to worship and praise our Lord. However, such a life seems impossible because sin has distorted our world. That is why the spiritual disciplines are essential to becoming spiritually mature.

For we see Paul say that God defeated sin and death through Christ (1 Cor. 15:56-57), therefore, we are no longer bound to sin and are free to live the life God intended for us. However, we know that this life is not easy and even though we have been freed there are still trials and temptations that hinder us from living this glorious life. So, to live out true spirituality, we must discipline ourselves spiritually, teaching our bodies to do what comes naturally to our spirit. As we pursue true spirituality, we pray that the "God of peace himself sanctify you completely, and may your whole spirit and soul and body be kept blameless at the coming of our Lord Jesus Christ." (1 Thess. 5:23). As we become more fully sanctified, we can live as we were intended, with God as the center of our life.

Questions for Further Thinking

What are your views on Spirituality? What are the cultural icons that are synonymous with spirituality? Are those correct?

Why is disciplining the body spiritually vital to us as believers today? If we are saved by grace, why do any works?

Prayer

God the Redeemer,
the right hand of Israel, the only true God:
Thank you for your love bestowed upon us; you have graciously given us the ability to pursue and actively discipline our bodies; we pray that we enter into life with you always at the center; give us the knowledge and strength today by day grow closer to you;
in the name of Jesus Christ, Amen.

THE WORK OF GRACE
Philippians 2:12-13
Andrew Barrett

"Well-informed human effort certainly is indispensable [to Christian spiritual formation], for spiritual formation is no passive process. But Christlikeness of the inner being is not a human attainment. It is, finally, a gift of grace." (*RH*, 23)

Intimacy requires work. We do not learn as much as there is to learn about someone simply by beginning a relationship with them. It takes time, intentionality, conversation, and so forth. I remember one evening where I could not find my wife in a restaurant, until I heard her *whistling*. I knew that was *her* whistle, and I was able to find where she had taken a seat. Being able to recognize her by her whistle requires countless hours of quality time; hearing her whistle and learning the particularities of her tone and cadence. If this is the case for human relations, how much more is it true between us and God. Now of course, God knows us. He knows us better than we know ourselves. God is, however, immeasurably knowable, and if part of our "salvation" involves deepening our knowledge of God until we "know fully, even as [we are] fully known" (1 Cor. 13:12), then work must be undertaken.

Our effort is *not* all that is required though, for our capacities are too limited. God works, too. The disciplines are, in fact, a sacrament: gifts of grace practiced by Jesus, preserved and handed down over generations of church history for the betterment of our relationship with the Father. Dependence on God's activity in these practices *he gave us* is key to our success, and Paul assures us that "it is God who works in you." God works in us as we devote time to him. How could he not? As our earthly parents delight in our getting to know them, so the heavenly Father delights in his children working to know him day by day. We have done nothing to earn these opportunities to know God deeper. Such is the gracious nature of the matter.

Questions for Further Thinking

How have you generally understood the assigned biblical passage? If Paul is not instructing us to *earn* our salvation, then how might we understand his words?

What disciplines/exercises/activities have you practiced to deepen your knowledge of God?

<u>Prayer</u>

Father,
who longs for us to know him and shows us how to do so;
We thank you that in Christ, Scripture, and the Great Tradition we have countless practices by which we may get to know you as you know us; resolve our discomfort with the idea of "work;" show us that the best relationships are the ones where the work has been put in;
in Jesus' name, Amen.

ACTING WITH GOD
Isaiah 64:8
Bohye Kim

"There arises a very real danger that we will set ourselves in opposition
to what God truly is doing now and aims to do in the future. Often we
miss the opportunity to act with God in the now." (*RH*, 21)

When an immediate situation in front of us provokes anxiety, terror, or
even anger, what is our initial reaction to it? Do we—like a child asking
"why"—inquire of God with multifaceted, suppressed emotions? Do we
tend to distance ourselves from God, instead of acting with God in the
now, and "set ourselves in opposition to what God truly is doing now?"[9]
Isn't anger the first reaction to an unwanted situation? Isn't frustration
and complaining the next response to it? This is my second attempt as
writing this devotion because I mistakenly deleted the first, beautifully
edited copy. Even after writing about "Acting with God," I quickly found
myself complaining. I was especially fond of today's devotion, for the
wording seemed appropriate and the flow felt smooth. The moment I
realized that my favorite devotion got deleted, I instantly put myself in
opposition to God, with complaint and frustration. My mind grumbled: 'I
poured so much time and effort into writing this devotion, but with a
blink of an eye, it disappeared. And there is no way to restore it. I even
called Apple Support, but they told me that restoring the file seemed
impossible.' Whenever we are in such disappointing situations, we often
we try to prove ourselves and fix the situation with our own strength,
despite our limited experience and wisdom. We often say a prayer like
this: "Dear God, either change the situation or my perception of the
circumstance." We often demand God to fix it. Instead of relying on his
power and acting with him on his side, we distance ourselves from God
and "set ourselves in opposition to what God truly is doing now."[10] (*RH*,
21) As I am writing exactly the same devotion twice at 11 pm—in which
I initially completed it at 11 am today—I am thankful that I got to
practice what I said. With a heart of contrition, I am practicing to "act
with God in the now." What a difficult and humbling practice.

---

[9] *RH*, 21.
[10] *RH*, 21.

Questions for Further Thinking

What are some ways in your lives that put us "in opposition to God," instead of "acting with God in the now"?

Read Isaiah 64:8 "Yet, O Lord, you are our Father; we are the clay, and you are our potter; we are all the work of your hand." Are you acknowledging God as your Father and potter and you as the clay? Are you willingly letting yourself to be the clay in the hands of the potter?

Prayer

Glorious Father,
you are the potter and I am the clay:
I praise you for giving us an opportunity to learn that we can act with you; form me in the way you want me to be; I want to be on your side acting with you, O God, instead of setting myself in opposition to you; renew my heart and my mind to humble myself before you;
through Jesus Christ our Lord, Amen.

WHAT DEFINES YOU?
1 John 3:9
Spencer Engelke

"Actions are not impositions on who we are, but are expressions of who we are. They come out of our heart and the inner realities it supervises and interacts with." (*RH*, 39)

When I was a kid, I would pretend to be all sorts of things: a dog, dinosaur, astronaut, etc. I would go the entire day walking on four legs, barking, even eating my plated food on the ground and lapping up water through a bowl. I would not talk, just woof and growl. I did nearly every possible action, albeit not every effort, to be a dog. However, no matter how good I was at acting like a dog, I could never be a dog. Why? The answer is obvious; biologically I have the DNA of a human. Thus, I cannot have the life of a canine. Now, that example is relatively easy to understand and recognize. Though, when it comes to our experience with God, it is not so easy. As believers there is innate pressure to act in a particular manner and behave in a certain way, which is justified. However, the problem arises when we as believers solely focus on our behavior and not our formation.

In 1 John 3:9 the text states, "No one born of God makes a practice of sinning, for God's seed, abides in him; and he cannot keep on sinning, because he has been born of God." Now, we can look at this verse in fear saying to ourselves, "I cannot have a practice of sin or I have not been born of God." That makes good logical sense, but it is missing the point of this verse and also is putting unwarranted pressure on us. The central message of this verse is that children of God are incapable of making a practice of sin solely because they have been born of God, it is not up to the children actions, but life is given to them by the Father. We may sin and make mistakes, but that does not contradict our nature. Just like my actions did not turn me into a dog, so our efforts do not turn us into children. In both instances, it is the life given to us that creates our identity.

Questions for Further Thinking

Have you felt as believers pressured to behave a certain way? Do that pressure stem from God forming you or a conforming out of your own will?

If our actions are an expression of who we are, rather than the substances of who we are, then where do we find our identity?

Prayer

Father God, the great I AM:
Thank you for being such a kind and loving Father; thank you for giving us life, life abundantly that will never run out; we praise you for never forsaking or departing from us; you are always amid our everyday lives, and we pray that we see you more clearly in that; please convict us to understand that we are children of God and that our nature draws us into things of you and not of this world;
in the name of Jesus Christ, Amen.

MYSTERIOUS EXPERIMENTATION
Luke 18:1-8
Andrew Barrett

"God's response to our prayers is not a charade. He does not pretend that he is answering our prayer when he is only doing what he was going to do anyway... The idea that everything would happen exactly as it does regardless of whether we pray or not is a specter that haunts the minds of many who sincerely profess belief in God. It makes prayer psychologically impossible, replacing it with dead ritual at best." (*DC*, 244)

Suppose a mother gives her children an allowance on Friday evening regardless of whether her children ask or not, and yet she still requires them to ask for it. The kids know that their mother will pay-up whether they ask or not, but they ask because that is just what they are supposed to do. What's more, the mother knows that the kids believe this way. "This," says Willard, "is the idea some people have of prayer."[11]

Willard's words are difficult. He is contradicting the way many of us have been taught to understand prayer. There is a tension here, of course, because I know that God will not simply give me everything I pray for. On the other hand, the great Scriptural scenes and instructions on prayer, including the one I have selected, invite the reader to see God as one who can be reasoned with and even impressed upon by our prayers. What we see is that prayer is a *mystery*; a mystery that we are invited to participate in and experiment with. Willard (and *Jesus!*) are inviting us to experiment with that part of the mystery of prayer that we are most uncomfortable with: that God may be convinced of things by our prayer; that our continual cries might compel God to act. I think that we will discover that when we pray in this way life with God feels much more like a genuine *life* than a set of rituals. We will sense that we are being listened to, considered, and responded to accordingly. We will learn to trust God, and prayer will seem less obligatory and more authentic. We will sense that we are indeed in a relationship.

---

[11] *DC,* 244. The illustration provided is an adaptation of Willard's own on the same page.

Questions for Further Thinking

In addition to the selected passage, read Exodus 32:9-14. How do you understand this passage in light of Willard's suggestion?

What difficulties have you had with prayer? How might you practice prayer in a ways that honors the mystery of prayer in Scripture?

Prayer

Father,
we are awestruck by the fact that you hear our prayers, even the ones we do not know to pray:
We confess that we do not understand prayer; we struggle to balance your affection for the needs of your children and your providential will; teach us to grow comfortable with mystery; kindle in us a trust that prayer matters; show us that you are a God we may delight in approaching in persistent prayer;
in Jesus' name. Amen.

IMPORTANCE OF FEELING
Proverbs 12:25
Bohye Kim

"...once we have given ourselves to Christ...[the task of the renovation of the heart] is to recognize the reality of our feelings and agree with the Lord to abandon those that are destructive and that leads us into doing or being what we know to be wrong." (*RH*, 137)

In the quote above, Dallas Willard articulates that the role of feelings in life is extremely vital for the renovation of our heart. Because feelings are powerful in two ways – as a blessing and a problem in our lives – it requires and deserves our careful attention. Feelings are intimately woven into our every day life, which affects the way we make decisions, view our surroundings, and treat others. For example, as a student, the worst emotion I can experience is disappointment whenever I receive a disappointing grade for a test or a paper. The very moment I check the grade which I did not expect, frustration dominates my feelings for that day. I can shake it off, think positively, and be more arduous in studying. However, as I allow this type of feeling, or in other words, lose control of such frustration, it captivates me by making it more important to my life than it really is. Being under such powerful feeling is an awful experience, for it affects my attitude toward God, my neighbors, and myself. I both knowingly and unconsciously express a degree of disappointment to them, like a porcupine ready to poke. This is not joy. It is definitely not being in the state of peace. I am not being present in God's perfect love, hope, and faith. As Willard advices, this is my recognition of the reality of my feeling, in front of my grade. What I need now is to *agree* with Jesus: *abandon* "those that are destructive," *receive* his holistic love, and be responsive to the love. How about you? How are you doing with your feelings?

Questions for Further Thinking

Dallas Willard underlines the importance of feeling, which has direct relation to our character change. Do feelings dominate your entire day? Do you allow feelings to control you, or do you control them?

How can you control your feelings? Do you think it is possible? What are some resources that can support your resist to a certain type of feeling?

<u>Prayer</u>

Father God,
you have created us in your perfect image:
We are created to receive your love; we are created to love you and our neighbors; I exult your name for inviting us to the community of perfect love; here I am fully accepting and receiving your love, and I surrender my feelings before your love; in the process of surrendering my feelings to the love of my father, help me to fully realize that I am loved by you; in Jesus' name, Amen.

OUR TRUE GOD
Luke 18:18-24
Spencer Engelke

"Jesus' word revealed his true god" (*SD*, 200)

In Luke 18 there is this story about a rich young ruler, who decides to walk up to Jesus and ask the simple question, "What must I do to inherit eternal life. Jesus, being God, decided to use this man's questions as a teaching point. Jesus tells the ruler what he wants to here, "You know the commandments: 'Do not commit adultery, Do not murder, Do not steal, Do not bear false witness, Honor your father and mother'" (Luke 18:20). To that, the ruler confidently expresses that he has kept all the commandments since his birth. Jesus then does not remand him for his arrogance but lovingly reveals that he lacks one thing, to sell all of his possessions and give the proceeds to the poor. Now, this appeal is the critical point of this passage, because Jesus is not mandating that to be saved everyone must sell everything, but showing that the ruler's true god was his possessions.

Now, this text can quickly be passed off as not applying to the reader, however that is a false assumption because we must all continually check if we are worshiping the true God, or if we are lording after a counterfeit god. We cannot experience the Lord and the Kingdom of here and now if we are not worshiping the true God. If our god is found in something other than the Lord, then we are destined to never experience God in the fullness and realness that God provides. The difficulty arises when we become so ingrained in idol worship that we do not even realize we are trading the glory of the Lord for images made by humankind (Romans 1:23). This endeavor is vital for our pursuit of Christ and can never be overlooked. For just as the rich young ruler walked away after discovering his fake god, so will we if we do not begin worshiping the true God.

Questions for Further Thinking

What is your true god? Are there things in your life that you are putting above the Lord? What can we do to combat that temptation?

How does worshiping the one true God affect the way we experience the Kingdom of God? Does our inability to worship God exclusively change the way we view the realness of the Kingdom?

Prayer

Lord Almighty,
the shepherd for the lost, the beginning and the end, the actual Creator: Thank you that we have the opportunity to experience You; we have been given more than we could ever realize and have been loved so intently; we pray today we put you on the throne and lay to waste the idols of our life; only through your strength and grace is that possible; so, God give us the endurance to run the race before us.
In the name of Jesus Christ, Amen.

GRACIOUS ENABLING
Psalm 1
Andrew Barrett

"The presence of the Spirit and of grace is not meant to set the law aside, but to enable conformity to it from an inwardly transformed personality. We walk in the spirit of the law and the letter naturally follows as is appropriate. You cannot separate spirit from law, though you must separate spirit *and* law from *legalism* – righteousness is terms of actions." (*RH*, 214)

Life with God is a *life* of grace dependency, from start to finish. God graciously redeems us so that, empowered by his Spirit, we may be people who delight in living out his law because of how good it is. The progression here is key: living out the law is not what draws us into Spirit-empowered life with God. Indeed it is impossible, because without the provision of God's resources we are helpless to live as he requires. We are accepted by God because of grace, but "Grace has to do with life, not just forgiveness."[12]

The psalmist is aware of this dynamic. The one who delights in God's law is "like a tree planted by streams of water" (1:3). The empowering sustenance the tree receives is outside of itself. The stream here is the grace of God, and the fruit is our good works – which we were created for (cf. Eph. 2:10) – enabled by such grace. Legalism is supposing that our production of fruit is what earns nutrients from the stream. If that idea sounds ridiculous, let those who have ears hear.

God's law, his instruction(s) for how we must orient our lives as his people, is only burdensome for the legalist who undertakes it without dependence on God. We stray from the biblical story when we contend that grace and the Spirit free us from the law as such. What we are freed from is the *burden* of the law, seeing it instead as utterly delightful, worthy of orienting our lives around, because it is a gift to us from God.

Questions for Further Thinking

---

[12] *RH*, 215.

Why did God give the law? Have you typically understood the law itself as a bad thing?

Read Ephesians 2:1-10, the read Psalm 1 once more. How do the texts help make sense out of each other?

<u>Prayer</u>

Father,
who not only invites us to live life with you, but shows us what that life should look like:
We confess that we have forsaken your law; we have failed to understand that by grace we are empowered to live your law as Jesus instructed; teach us to confide in you not only for forgiveness but for life; mold us into one like the psalmist, who sees your law as delightful;
in the name of Jesus, who came not to abolish the law but to fulfill it, Amen.

OUR HEART BEFORE GOD
1 John 3:19-20
Bohye Kim

"To God the amazing duplicity of the human heart is totally transparent…Our only hope is to entirely place our confidence in the God and Father of Jesus Christ, who is willing to enter the duplicity of our heart and bring it wholly to himself if we earnestly invite him." (*RH*, 148)

We intellectually understand that God is omniscient (all-knowing) and omnipotent (all-powerful), but are we actually aware that God meticulously sees our hearts *in this moment*? Our hearts are "totally transparent" before him. It was not only transparent in the past when we first confessed Jesus Christ as our savior or when we got baptized. God will not only know it before our last breath in the coming future. The transparency of our heart in front of God is in the present tense, active voice. It is *now* being scrupulously watched, searched, and tested. Whenever we are calm and composed, it is easier to yield in awful traffic. On the other hand, when there are layers of distraction and discontentment in life, it is easier to express uneasiness or complaining attitude toward a person cutting in line. The duplicity of our heart is amazing, as Willard highlights. The purpose of underlining the transparency of our heart before God is not to cause creepiness, fear, or condemnation but to emphasize God's nearness, who observes and waits our hearts to give undivided attention to God. Happy news from Willard is that God is very "sensitive to the slightest move of the heart."[13] If our heart moves closer toward God even in the slightest sense, God rejoices!

What is it that makes us forget that God sees through our heart? In the quote above Willard gives us a hint in the form of a question: Have we "earnestly" invited him to fix the duplicity of our heart? My answer was "No." The way I responded regarding to my duplicity of heart was embarrassment and qualm, and that was it. Instead of proactively welcoming and allowing God to transform my heart, I just stood there abashed in shame. Now that I know what to do with the "amazing

---

[13] *RH*, 148.

duplicity" of my heart, I find confidence in God and find hope in him who is "greater than [my] heart." (1 John 3:20)

Questions for Further Thinking

How did you react to the "amazing duplicity" of your heart?

Did you try to fix the duplicity of heart on your own? Was it helpful and effective?

Prayer

Father God,
you lovingly search through our heart:
We gladly invite you to touch upon our heart; grant us grace and joy in the process of aligning our heart to you;
in the name of Jesus, Amen.

THE UNESCAPABLE
Romans 3:23
Spencer Engelke

"One of the greatest obstacles of effective spiritual formation in Christ today is simple failure to understand and acknowledge the reality of the human situation as it affects Christians and non-Christians alike." (*RH,* 45)

We do not choose to be formed spiritually; it is not up to our compliance. We will be established no matter our indigitation or enticement. Being spiritually formed is not exclusively for the elite, mature, poor, immature, or any class in this world; it happens to every single human being. That is because as human beings we must interact with our surroundings, so that through people, the environment, the tv, etc. we are being developed and influenced every single day. So, the question is not *if* I am spiritually formed, but *what* is spiritually forming me? We must understand this first principle because once we conclude that we are spiritually formed, we can focus our intention on being correctly developed. However, that is where Romans 3:23 comes into great value, for it is necessary to know that because of sin we as human beings are distorted, we need saving. Once we come to that realization, we begin to understand why sin is so detrimental to our lives, because if we are being formed by sin, then we will replicate the effects of sin (death, destruction, etc.) in our soul, which is one of the great hindrances to our pursuit of the Lord.

Now that we understand the effects of sin in our formations the redemption of Christ becomes vastly more significate. For we were not only saved for eternal perdition when we die but are given an ability to be spiritually formed by the grace of God and not sin. If we now have the knowledge and the recognition of the need for real and proper spiritual formation by God, we can now live a life in the manner worthy of our Lord, not by our actions but by the grace bestowed on us from God. We can now be a part of the Kingdom of God here and now, allowing God to have dominion over our lives and choosing to be formed by God's great love.

Questions for Further Thinking

What is spiritual formation? Why are we spiritually formed regardless of our compliance?

What is sin? Why does sin have a negative effect on our lives? How can we practically choose to be formed by God and not sin?

Prayer

Father God,
you are worthy of every sacrifice, praise, or offering we could give:
You give hope to the hopeless; you love the unworthy; you care for the forgotten; you house the homeless; you provide comfort to the broken; thank you for all your goodness; there is none like you, and we want to announce that your name is above all others; allow us to be formed by your kindness and faithfulness;
In the name of Jesus Christ, Amen.

ATTENTIVE DISTRACTION
1 Kings 8
Andrew Barrett

"What characterizes most of our local congregations, whether big or little in size, is simple distraction. The oft-noted 'failures' of many kinds that show up within them and around them are not the fundamental problem of church life today. They are much more a result than a cause" (*RH*, 235)

It is the eighth day, and the people are returning home from the party of all parties. Solomon completed the construction of God's temple, the glory of the Lord filled the Holy Place, Solomon pronounced a blessing followed by a joyous benediction, innumerable sacrifices were offered, and a feast was held. It was a day of worship like no other.

Suppose two friends were reflecting on this occasion, and one of them mentioned that while he enjoyed most of it, he wished that Solomon would not have been so repetitive in his prayer. His complaint may sound ridiculous, but such comments are made after church services every week. How many times has God acted mightily among us, only to go unnoticed because of some problem we had with the music or the reading. These, Willard argues, are distractions.

God is the active agent in this life we share with him. Our worship is a response to what he is doing; what he is teaching us. My wife is a teacher, and we have conversed many times on how much better off her students would be if they were not so distracted during instructional time. The students often ask questions about something my wife *just* taught about, but they missed it, not because it wasn't discussed, but because they were distracted. Such is the case in many of our spiritual lives. God is not inactive; we are inattentive, distracted by matters of little importance. When we fix our gaze on what God is up to, everything else will fall into place. In our passage, the party begins when God moves: he occupies the Holy Place and the celebration is *on!* When the people of God pay attention to the work of God, it is impossible to leave that place dissatisfied.

Questions for Further Thinking

Can you recall a time you noticed God working during either your personal or corporate worship?

Consider the most recent worship service you attended. When you reflected on the service (*if* you reflected on the service), what was the first thing you discussed?

Prayer

God,
who is busy at work in the world, and in our lives;
We are inattentive children; we confess that your works go unnoticed in our lives because of our distractedness; fix our gaze on you; teach us to bear with matters of secondary importance, because what matters is what you are up to;
in Jesus' name, Amen.

GOD'S DEEP INTEREST IN OUR HEART
Jeremiah 17:10
Bohye Kim

"The heart (will, spirit) is precisely what God observes and addresses in human beings…he is sensitive to the slightest move of the heart." (*RH*, 148)

Have you ever thought that your slightest transformation of heart makes God very happy? Whenever we move a step closer to God, he is not inactive. Rather, he gladly observes our movement toward him. We have grown accustomed to an image of God, where he is an angry grandfather who punishes his children to teach them a lesson: to return to Him. This is such a forceful image of God to have. Dallas Willard's keen observation of God's reaction to our heart's movement toward him tells us that we serve a God who truly rejoices when his prodigal children return home and refocus their heart to God. It is because, as Willard quotes above, God "observes and addresses" to us through our heart. Jeremiah 17:10 says, "I the Lord search the heart and test the mind, to give every man according to his ways, according to the fruit of his deeds." We learn from the author of Jeremiah that God enthusiastically hears and reacts to our heart without failing. Even in Deuteronomy 6:5, God commands us to love him with all our *heart,* soul, and might. God's whole focus is on our heart.

It is the heart that God wants from us. God is deeply interested in our heart. He is not interested in how we look, what our degree is, what our occupation is, what our social status is, or of our skin color. Peter, in Acts 10:34, understands that "God shows no partiality," but for those who fearfully make movement toward him. He is definitely attracted to the movement of your heart and my heart.

Questions for Further Thinking

How can we be responsible of our movement of heart?

What is the condition of the heart that is with God?

Prayer

Loving God,
your overflowing love has captivated our heart:
We are here moving closer to you daily; thank you for letting us know
that you are passionate about our heart; grant us the fullness of joy when
our heart is moving closer to you;
in Jesus' name, Amen.

GOD HEARS
Psalm 34:15
Spencer Engelke

"No great sophistication or information about God is required to be reached by God."
(*RH*, 149)

A man brought a boy that was demon possessed to Jesus. He stated that the demon caused the boy to be mute and would throw him on the ground. The man, in apparent disarray, asks Jesus if he can, to please heal the boy. Jesus replies that with belief all things are possible. The man, with reckless abandon, then shouts, "I believe help my unbelief," and after that confession, Jesus casts out the demon (Mark 9:14-25). This prayer was simple, though it had major ramifications. Sometimes we believe that we must possess a profound knowledge of God for God to hear our prayers. However, that cannot be farther from the truth. In Psalm 34:15 the text states, "The eyes of the Lord are toward the righteous and his ears toward their cry." When people cry to the Lord, regardless of circumstance, God not only hears but sees them. There is no prerequisite for prayer but faith, faith that God can and will provide. We do not need to obtain knowledge somehow so that we can reach God; we do not need to study hours upon hours to reach God; we merely have to cry out to God.

Just as the man did not have a complete understanding of who Jesus was, asking if Jesus was able, God still heard and granted the man's provision. Not because the man said the magic words, or finally understood who Jesus was, but because he was utterly reliant in God. When we focus our attention on our efforts, then we miss the point of God's love. God's love is so amazing because it is a free gift. We bring our unrighteousness, and he lavishes on us grace and peace. To reach God is just dependent on believing in God, that is it.

Questions for Further Thinking

Why do some view prayer as a magic spell? That in order to reach God they have to say the right words?

Think about the man with the demon-possessed boy, have you ever felt yourself in a situation like that? Did your response with a focus on your efforts or just threw yourself at the mercy of God?

Prayer

God Almighty,
you are right, and you cannot be praised enough:
Our works of righteous our but filthy grabs compared to your everlasting glory; you are worthy of all nothing, no one measures up to you and your mercy; you are above all and in all; thank you for your gift of knowledge; let us not worship knowing of you, but know you personally; allow us to be formed by your goodness and faithfulness;
in the name of Jesus Christ, Amen.

BURRIED TREASURE
Matthew 13:45-46
Andrew Barrett

"The most important commandment of the Judeo-Christian tradition is to treasure God and his realm more than anything else. That is what it means to love God with all your heart, soul, mind, and strength. It means to *treasure* him, to hold him and his dear, and to protect and aid him in his purposes." (*DC,* 203)

"Treasures," Willard continues, "are directly connected to our spirit, or will."[14] Life with God involves orienting our will around the will of the Father. We aspire to, like Jesus, have a will that is synchronized with our Father in heaven. Many of us have attempted to undertake this lifestyle, only to discover that it is difficult and – for some of us – undoable. That is because we have misunderstood the process. We cannot work ourselves into a transformed heart. The man in our selected parable only sells his field *after* he discovered the treasure in the field.

Such is the order of the transformed life with God: We understand that there are no treasures more worthy of our devotion than Almighty God. With God as our treasure, our heart follows suit. When our heart sets out in the direction of God, the life we have so struggled to live naturally follows suit. Jesus' parable lacks a period of discernment. The man does not struggle to decide whether or not his field is more valuable than the treasure. He *immediately* sells it all. That was the natural response.

The hard reality here is that if our spirit or will is taking us to a place contrary to the kingdom of God, it is likely the case that God's kingdom is not our treasure. "Have you understood all these things?" Jesus asks (Matt. 13:51). The heart is where the treasure is (6:21), and our lives are the results of our heart's location.

Questions for Further Thinking

---

[14] *DC,* 203.

What "properties" of yours do you have trouble surrendering for God and his kingdom?

How do you respond to the notion that – when God is our true treasure – the life of obedience to him is easier?

<u>Prayer</u>

Father,
whose beauty and worth surpasses all would-be treasures of the world;
We confess that we have treated you as one of many earthly treasures;
contrary to the man in the parable, we attempt to secure the treasure *and* keep the field; cleanse us of such idolatry; show us that there is no authentic life where the heart is not;
this we beg you in Jesus' name, Amen.

IT IS GOOD TO BE NEAR GOD
Psalm 73:28
Bohye Kim

"My soul is at peace only when it is with God." (*RH*, 209)

In the 21st Century, an era of postmodernism, the remnants of human instinct to satiate their thirst still remain in different and advanced forms, which never fully succeed in quenching their thirst. Blaise Pascal gives a better language about this perspective of unsatisfied craving in *Pensees*: "What else does this craving, and this helplessness, proclaim but that there was once in man a true happiness, of which all that now remains is the empty print and trace? This he tries in vain to fill with everything around him, seeking in things that are not there the help he cannot find in those that are though none can help, since this infinite abyss can be filled only...by God."[15]

As Dallas Willard confesses, our soul can be at peace only when it is *with* its Creator. When we need peace, do we decide to *be with* God, or do we run for other substantial things? To quench a sense of thirst and need, we often reach out to material benefits, money, fame, debauchery, sex, sports, addiction, or any kind of temporary things that provide an instant pleasure. These deceitfully make us to be unaware of its nonpermanent state, for it provides a sense of enjoyment right away. We are often reminded on Sunday mornings at church that our soul can be at peace when it is with our heavenly Father. Think about our reaction. We nod as we hear it from the pastor, write it down in journal, and think that it is important. That is good. However, how much do we actually assent and intentionally find God to find true peace? During the week, do we ever speculate on the things that we tend to find peace in? Whenever I am stressed out, I tend to play violin because its high and sharp tones give me a sense of relief of stress. Do I run to God, kneel down and pray to allow my soul to be with God? My honest answer is, "Not always." The psalmist already knew that being near with God was the answer for life: "But for me it is good to be near God; I have made the Lord God my

---

[15] Blaise Pascal. *Pensées*. trans. A. J. Krailsheimer (New York: Penguin Books, 1966), 75.

refuge, that I may tell of all your works." (Psalm 73:28). After realizing over and over again that true peace is found in God, whenever I am in need of peace, I begin talking to him, honestly expressing my thoughts and emotions to him. Soon, a gentle peace quietly lands in my heart.

Questions for Further Thinking

What is your first reaction to lack of peace?

What is your way to be with God?

Prayer

Heavenly Father,
you love us so much that you only allow true peace when we are with you:
We thank you for your strong love that calls us all the time; help us to be responsive to your love, and remind us that it is good to be near you;
in Jesus' name, Amen.

GOD WANTS ALL OF YOU
1 Thessalonians 5:23
Spencer Engelke

"The way to a life filled and fruitful with goodness is the transformation of every dimension of the inner or "spiritual" side of self." (*RH*, 222)

Paul claims that your whole body, soul, and spirit be sanctified to the uttermost (1 Thess. 5:23). Sometimes we tend to focus our attention on one thing in our spiritual lives, our moral and ethical behavior. We devote so much attention to our action that we forget or neglect the other dimensions of our self. Though, as the entire Bible points out, God wants all of you. Not just your funds, not only your time, behavior, etc. but every single facet of your life. For then you will live a life filled to the entirety of how the Lord created. Unfortunately, there is this notion in Christianity that sanctification is optional or that being redeemed to the uttermost is unattainable. We must fight against those notions for the sake of our souls. Our souls long to be confirmed and reoriented towards the Lord.

Anything that we do that is not of the Lord leads to death. Romans 6:23 is explicit when saying, "the wages of sin is death." Not just death in the sense of eternal judgment but dying in the mind. When we pursue and commit sin, we are distancing ourselves from God our ultimate supply of life. In order to achieve the easy yoke Christ promises (Matt. 11:30), we must choose life. We must begin to have all of the facets of our self: mind, body, soul, will, and social conformed to Christ. That is when complete spiritual transformation occurs, and our entire body, soul, and spirit are sanctified.

Questions for Further Thinking

Why do we tend to focus our attention on our actions when highlighting spiritual growth? Did it surprise you how much more spiritual growth is than simply behaving right?

What dimensions of yourself listed above (mind, body, soul, will, and social) do you find the easiest to discipline spiritually? Which ones are more difficult?

Prayer

Heavenly Father,
the great I AM, the one who knows all, the greatest one in history:
We praise you; thank you for the gift of sanctification; we want to grow closer to you in the entirety of our self; please grace us the ability to pursue your life to the uttermost; Lord, allow us to experience your love and grace as an avenue into your Kingdom; you are the one worthy of all praise;
Thank you. In the name of Jesus Christ, Amen.

PRACTICE MAKES PEACE
Philippians 4:6-7
Andrew Barrett

"The secret to this peace is, as great apprentices of Jesus have long known, *being abandoned to God...* the person who is heartily abandoned to God knows that all shall be well because God is in charge of his or her life. My peace is the greatness of God." (*RH,* 135)

The progression of Paul's language in Philippians 4 is indicative of Willard words here. Having received the incomprehensible peace of God – that is, having abandoned himself and his need to control the outcome(s) of his life – Paul is able to be content in all circumstances (4:11).

We have said much over the course of these reflections on the *order* of the spiritual life, and I am afraid this installment is not any different. There is an enormous tendency in Christian circles to cite Philippians 4:13 in the context of grinding out something that we do not wish to do, but know that we should.[16] Such use of the verse, however, misunderstands the biblical context. Paul is confident that he can do all things – that he can be content in good or bad circumstances – because his life of spiritual formation has established the peace of God within him. He has become a man of unshakable peace, because he has abandoned control to God, trusting that, as he will write elsewhere, "for those who love God all things work together for good" (Rom. 8:28).

This peace is not received quickly. Paul's promise of peace comes in the context of a call to consistent, meticulous prayer. Over and against being anxious about our lives – indicating our need to control outcomes – we are called to take everything to God in prayer. As we do so, we learn to confide in God more and more until our lives are shaped into one of confidence, self-abandonment, and contentment. If Paul's words here seem impossible, it is not because he is exaggerating, but because we have not tested his proposition.

---

[16] Never mind the vast misuse of this text in popular culture.

Questions for Further Thinking

What parts of your life do you *not* typically pray about? Why do you think you do not bother praying about them?

How have you typically understood things like "peace" or "contentment"? Do you view these things are something that we *do,* or – in a sense – something that we *are*?

Prayer

God,
whose peace surpasses all understanding:
We confess that much of our angst is due to our failure to trust you; we do not abandon ourselves or our outcomes to you, because we have not committed to you; teach us to order our spiritual lives rightly; show us that contentment comes *after* receiving your peace, not before; we are a worn out and stressed people; draw us to you in prayer; in Jesus' name, Amen.

Bibliography

Willard, Dallas. *Renovation of the Heart: Putting on the Character of Christ.* Colorado Springs: NavPress, 2002.

Willard, Dallas. *The Divine Conspiracy: Rediscovering Our Hidden Life in God.* San Francisco: HarperSanFrancisco, 1997.

Willard, Dallas. *The Spirit of the Disciplines: Understanding How God Changes Lives.* San Francisco: HarperSanFrancisco, 1988.

Pascal, Blaise. *Pensées.* trans. A. J. Krailsheimer. New York: Penguin Books, 1966.

Printed in Great Britain
by Amazon

80917774R00058